Published by Maria Christina Schultz
Fredericksburg, Va., USA

MariaChristinaSchultz.com

ISBN: 978-0-578-44819-0

Cover design and book design by Maria Christina Schultz. Edited by Lisa Chinn Marvashti. Cover photo, Maria Schultz and Kona.

Disclaimers:
The purpose of this book is to inspire others to try similar activities with their dogs. The author is not a veterinarian and is not qualified to offer medical advice. Anyone wishing to participate in any dog related activity should be physically prepared, and seek training advice from a professional trainer or instructor first. The author and publisher are not liable for any adverse effects or injuries you or your dog may experience from the information contained in this book. Outdoor activities can be risky and should be entered into with caution.

My Dog and Me

This book belongs to:

_____ & _____

Because every dog has his day... but they all deserve hundreds!

I couldn't have a dog growing up, but nothing could stop me from reading about them. Sled dogs, police dogs, Seeing Eye dogs ... I couldn't get enough.

Week after week, I'd return my favorite collection of dog stories to the Colonial Village Library, only to turn around and check it back out again. I can still hear the crinkle of its cellophane jacket, smell the musty worn pages, see that card tucked into the back-cover pocket, filled from front to back with only my name on each of its lines.

But Mom made it clear: Dogs deserve tons of attention. If we wanted one, we'd need to commit completely to taking care of it. It wouldn't be fair to leave it at home alone. My three siblings and I were simply told, "You'll just have to wait until you grow up."

When I did grow up, and finally had a house of my own and a job with an easy commute, I knew it was time.

Riley, my first Australian shepherd, was the dog I'd been waiting for all of my life. Addicted to his puppy breath, enamored by his silly nature, in love with his blue eyes and splotchy brown coat, I left him alone as little as possible. On those rare occasions when I did leave the house without him, Mom's words would ring through my head, and I started bringing him everywhere! We chose restaurants with outdoor seating and dog-friendly hotels. I'd even sneak him into the office whenever I could.

When Riley was 5, we got some bad news. We learned he had hip dysplasia, and though I was well into my 30s, I cried for a week. The dog I had longed for forever might have to bow out of our action-packed life much earlier than I had imagined. The diagnosis moved me to start finding even more ways to make each day count, to include Riley in every facet of my life.

Then we got lucky. Despite the X-rays, he continued to thrive, and six years later, he'd collected an impressive list of accomplishments. He'd become a big brother to our second dog Kona, gotten certified as a therapy dog, hiked to the highestpoint in his home state, came nose to nose with a manatee, herded sheep, appeared on magazine covers, helped me write a book, driven across half the country and paddled all five Great Lakes with me, the list goes on and on.

Then, when he was 11, I found a tumor on Riley's muzzle. The vet seemed certain it was cancerous, so I wasted no time scheduling surgery. Once again, Riley's luck held — the growth was benign!

My overwhelming sense of relief was only rivaled by the thoughts that I'd had in the weeks leading up to his surgery. My lucky, once-in-a-lifetime dog had done so much, but I hadn't taken the time to record my thoughts about many of our treasured adventures. I wondered what other fantastic things we could still do and see in our time together, and I made up my mind to write and journal about all of them.

Our adventures together have enriched Riley's life, yes, but it's not just about him. They've also helped me, filling my heart with happiness and joy as we've navigated this world side by side, along with Kona.

I believe that every dog deserves a life like Riley's and Kona's and that every dog deserves his very own bucket list.

It's true: Every dog does have his day. I hope this book helps you and your dog plan hundreds of them!

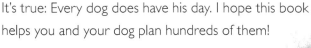

ROLLING IN THE GRASS ON A WARM SUMMER DAY IS ONE OF RILEY'S FAVORITE THINGS!

How to use this book

Riley's list of adventures is quite ambitious! He's an athletic, confident, well-behaved dog who can easily do things other dogs might struggle with. To make your bucket list unique, especially designed for you and your dog, here are a few things to keep in mind:

- Not all dogs enjoy the same activities. Think about what your dog actually likes versus what you *want* him to like, and try to choose activities you'll both enjoy.

- Consider the history of your breed. For example, if you have a husky and you live in the South, perhaps a trip north in the winter to play in the snow should be on your list!

- Not all adventures need to be big. Small, simple outings can be meaningful, too. Adventuring locally can be just as fulfilling as driving all the way across the country!

- When trying something new with your dog, always consider how to prepare him for the experience. Something like learning how to kayak together may take a few weeks of training and confidence-building before you ever hit the water.

- **Everything starts with basic obedience and socialization**! A solid foundation gives dogs a better chance of successfully navigating the world at your side and handling new sights, sounds and environments. Training works better when dogs are young, but old dogs can learn new tricks, too, so don't pass up the opportunity to spend time with an older rescue. It's never too late to start exploring the world together.

This book's four sections will help you generate ideas for experiences to share with your dog:

1 PLACES WE WANT TO VISIT.
Maybe it's a local park or even a national park, or maybe it's just an outdoor restaurant. Wherever you decide to go, check to make sure it's dog friendly ahead of time!

2 ACTIVITIES AND SKILLS WE WANT TO LEARN TOGETHER.
What will make your dog smile and get you both moving? Running a 5k? Mastering an agility course? Dock diving? You could even consider something as simple as springing for that end-of-the-summer Doggie Dive at your local pool.

3 GOALS WE WANT TO ACHIEVE.
Training for things like obedience titles and therapy work is a great way to bond with your dog. Ever thought about herding sheep?

4 JUST BECAUSE WE CAN.
This section is where you and your dog can really have fun. Think bacon, mud, and all things messy and stinky! Ruff!!

Remember, this book is *yours*. Make it work for you and your dog, and most importantly, have fun!

#NoDogLeftAtHome

Here's a sample from our bucket list to get you started!

PADDLEBOARD WITH MANATEES

☑

COMPLETED

12/27/17

DATE

Paddleboard with Manatees!

WHY WE WANT TO DO THIS I've had a lifelong fascination with marine life and dogs. Manatees are gentle and curious, and so are my dogs. I belive their training is solid enough for this adventure - plus they love making new friends!

WHAT DOES MY DOG NEED TO KNOW FOR THIS ADVENTURE? Riley and Kona both need to stay on the board under the most distracting circumstances. We also need a backup plan in case the dogs or manatees show sings of stress.

SUMMARY OF THE DAY We must have seen 50! Riley and Kona were as curious about the manatees as the manatees were of them! They inquisitively peered over the rails to watch the sea cows play, swim and push our board. I could even see their small black eyes trying to get a closer look at the dogs. Riley got his nose a few inches from one almost getting a kiss! Watching my dogs respectfully observe the manatees with me was remarkable. I'm so proud of them for being so well-behaved!

FUN SCALE:

1 BISCUIT OF FUN

10 BISCUITS OF FUN

VISIT ALL THE LIGHTHOUSES ON THE EAST COAST

1

Places we want to visit

DRIVE ACROSS THE COUNTRY TOGETHER

SEE A DRIVE-IN MOVIE

ROMP ON AN OFF-LEASH DOG BEACH

WATCH THE SUN RISE ON THE EAST COAST,
AND THE SUN SET ON THE WEST COST

1

_____

_____

_____

☐

COMPLETED

DATE

WHY WE WANT TO DO THIS _____

_____

_____

_____

WHAT DOES MY DOG NEED TO KNOW FOR THIS ADVENTURE? _____

_____

_____

_____

SUMMARY OF THE DAY _____

_____

_____

_____

_____

_____

_____

_____

_____

FUN SCALE:

1 BISCUIT OF FUN   10 BISCUITS OF FUN

☐

COMPLETED

_____

DATE

2

_____
_____
_____
_____

WHY WE WANT TO DO THIS _____
_____
_____
_____
_____

WHAT DOES MY DOG NEED TO KNOW FOR THIS ADVENTURE? _____
_____
_____
_____
_____

SUMMARY OF THE DAY _____
_____
_____
_____
_____
_____
_____
_____
_____
_____

FUN SCALE:

1 BISCUIT OF FUN   10 BISCUITS OF FUN

3

_____
_____
_____

☐
COMPLETED

....
DATE

WHY WE WANT TO DO THIS
_____
_____
_____
_____

WHAT DOES MY DOG NEED TO KNOW FOR THIS ADVENTURE?
_____
_____
_____

SUMMARY OF THE DAY
_____
_____
_____
_____
_____
_____
_____
_____

FUN SCALE:

1 BISCUIT OF FUN   10 BISCUITS OF FUN

☐

COMPLETED

_____

DATE

4

WHY WE WANT TO DO THIS

WHAT DOES MY DOG NEED TO KNOW FOR THIS ADVENTURE?

SUMMARY OF THE DAY

FUN SCALE:

1 BISCUIT OF FUN   10 BISCUITS OF FUN

5

_____
_____
_____
_____

WHY WE WANT TO DO THIS _____
_____
_____
_____

WHAT DOES MY DOG NEED TO KNOW FOR THIS ADVENTURE? _____
_____
_____
_____

SUMMARY OF THE DAY _____
_____
_____
_____
_____
_____
_____
_____
_____

FUN SCALE:

1 BISCUIT OF FUN   10 BISCUITS OF FUN

☐

COMPLETED

_____

DATE

6

WHY WE WANT TO DO THIS _____

_____

_____

_____

WHAT DOES MY DOG NEED TO KNOW FOR THIS ADVENTURE? _____

_____

_____

_____

SUMMARY OF THE DAY _____

_____

_____

_____

_____

_____

_____

_____

_____

_____

FUN SCALE:

1 BISCUIT OF FUN   10 BISCUITS OF FUN

7

_____

_____

_____

_____

☐

COMPLETED

DATE

WHY WE WANT TO DO THIS _____

_____

_____

_____

WHAT DOES MY DOG NEED TO KNOW FOR THIS ADVENTURE? _____

_____

_____

_____

SUMMARY OF THE DAY _____

_____

_____

_____

_____

_____

_____

_____

_____

_____

FUN SCALE:

1 BISCUIT OF FUN

10 BISCUITS OF FUN

COMPLETED

DATE

8

WHY WE WANT TO DO THIS

WHAT DOES MY DOG NEED TO KNOW FOR THIS ADVENTURE?

SUMMARY OF THE DAY

FUN SCALE:

1 BISCUIT OF FUN   10 BISCUITS OF FUN

9

☐

COMPLETED

DATE

WHY WE WANT TO DO THIS

WHAT DOES MY DOG NEED TO KNOW FOR THIS ADVENTURE?

SUMMARY OF THE DAY

FUN SCALE:

1 BISCUIT OF FUN

10 BISCUITS OF FUN

☐

COMPLETED

DATE

10

WHY WE WANT TO DO THIS

WHAT DOES MY DOG NEED TO KNOW FOR THIS ADVENTURE?

SUMMARY OF THE DAY

FUN SCALE:

1 BISCUIT OF FUN   10 BISCUITS OF FUN

11

_____

_____

_____

WHY WE WANT TO DO THIS _____

_____

_____

_____

WHAT DOES MY DOG NEED TO KNOW FOR THIS ADVENTURE? _____

_____

_____

_____

SUMMARY OF THE DAY _____

_____

_____

_____

_____

_____

_____

_____

_____

_____

FUN SCALE:

1 BISCUIT OF FUN   10 BISCUITS OF FUN

GO HIKING IN ALL THE DOG-FRIENDLY NATIONAL PARKS

12

_____
_____
_____

☐
COMPLETED

DATE

WHY WE WANT TO DO THIS _____
_____
_____
_____

WHAT DOES MY DOG NEED TO KNOW FOR THIS ADVENTURE? _____
_____
_____
_____

SUMMARY OF THE DAY _____
_____
_____
_____
_____
_____
_____
_____
_____

FUN SCALE:

1 BISCUIT OF FUN   10 BISCUITS OF FUN

☐

COMPLETED

....

DATE

13

WHY WE WANT TO DO THIS

_____

_____

_____

_____

WHAT DOES MY DOG NEED TO KNOW FOR THIS ADVENTURE?

_____

_____

_____

SUMMARY OF THE DAY

_____

_____

_____

_____

_____

_____

_____

_____

FUN SCALE:

1 BISCUIT OF FUN   10 BISCUITS OF FUN

14

☐

COMPLETED

DATE

WHY WE WANT TO DO THIS

WHAT DOES MY DOG NEED TO KNOW FOR THIS ADVENTURE?

SUMMARY OF THE DAY

FUN SCALE:

1 BISCUIT OF FUN

10 BISCUITS OF FUN

☐

COMPLETED

_____

DATE

15

WHY WE WANT TO DO THIS _____

_____

_____

_____

WHAT DOES MY DOG NEED TO KNOW FOR THIS ADVENTURE? _____

_____

_____

_____

SUMMARY OF THE DAY _____

_____

_____

_____

_____

_____

_____

_____

_____

_____

FUN SCALE:

1 BISCUIT OF FUN   10 BISCUITS OF FUN

16

_____

_____

_____

_____

WHY WE WANT TO DO THIS _____

_____

_____

_____

WHAT DOES MY DOG NEED TO KNOW FOR THIS ADVENTURE? _____

_____

_____

_____

SUMMARY OF THE DAY _____

_____

_____

_____

_____

_____

_____

_____

_____

_____

FUN SCALE:

1 BISCUIT OF FUN   10 BISCUITS OF FUN

☐

COMPLETED

....

DATE

17

WHY WE WANT TO DO THIS _____

_____

_____

_____

_____

WHAT DOES MY DOG NEED TO KNOW FOR THIS ADVENTURE? _____

_____

_____

_____

_____

SUMMARY OF THE DAY _____

_____

_____

_____

_____

_____

_____

_____

_____

_____

_____

FUN SCALE:

1 BISCUIT OF FUN   10 BISCUITS OF FUN

18

_____

_____

_____

....
DATE

WHY WE WANT TO DO THIS _____

_____

_____

_____

WHAT DOES MY DOG NEED TO KNOW FOR THIS ADVENTURE? _____

_____

_____

_____

SUMMARY OF THE DAY _____

_____

_____

_____

_____

_____

_____

_____

_____

FUN SCALE:

1 BISCUIT OF FUN   10 BISCUITS OF FUN

☐

COMPLETED

_____

DATE

19

_____
_____
_____
_____

WHY WE WANT TO DO THIS _____

_____
_____
_____
_____

WHAT DOES MY DOG NEED TO KNOW FOR THIS ADVENTURE? _____

_____
_____
_____
_____

SUMMARY OF THE DAY _____

_____
_____
_____
_____
_____
_____
_____
_____
_____
_____

FUN SCALE: 🦴 🦴 🦴 🦴 🦴 🦴 🦴 🦴 🦴 🦴

1 BISCUIT OF FUN   10 BISCUITS OF FUN

20

_____

_____

_____

☐

COMPLETED

DATE

WHY WE WANT TO DO THIS _____

_____

_____

_____

WHAT DOES MY DOG NEED TO KNOW FOR THIS ADVENTURE? _____

_____

_____

_____

SUMMARY OF THE DAY _____

_____

_____

_____

_____

_____

_____

_____

_____

FUN SCALE: 🦴 🦴 🦴 🦴 🦴 🦴 🦴 🦴 🦴 🦴

1 BISCUIT OF FUN   10 BISCUITS OF FUN

☐

COMPLETED

_____

DATE

21

WHY WE WANT TO DO THIS _____

_____

_____

_____

WHAT DOES MY DOG NEED TO KNOW FOR THIS ADVENTURE? _____

_____

_____

_____

SUMMARY OF THE DAY _____

_____

_____

_____

_____

_____

_____

_____

_____

FUN SCALE: 🦴 🦴 🦴 🦴 🦴 🦴 🦴 🦴 🦴 🦴

1 BISCUIT OF FUN   10 BISCUITS OF FUN

22

☐ COMPLETED

DATE

WHY WE WANT TO DO THIS

_____

WHAT DOES MY DOG NEED TO KNOW FOR THIS ADVENTURE?

_____

SUMMARY OF THE DAY

_____

FUN SCALE:

1 BISCUIT OF FUN   10 BISCUITS OF FUN

□

COMPLETED

——————————

DATE

23

WHY WE WANT TO DO THIS

WHAT DOES MY DOG NEED TO KNOW FOR THIS ADVENTURE?

SUMMARY OF THE DAY

FUN SCALE:

1 BISCUIT OF FUN

10 BISCUITS OF FUN

24

_____
_____
_____
_____

WHY WE WANT TO DO THIS

_____
_____
_____
_____

WHAT DOES MY DOG NEED TO KNOW FOR THIS ADVENTURE?

_____
_____
_____
_____

SUMMARY OF THE DAY

_____
_____
_____
_____
_____
_____
_____
_____
_____

FUN SCALE:

1 BISCUIT OF FUN   10 BISCUITS OF FUN

☐

COMPLETED

_____

DATE

_____

25

WHY WE WANT TO DO THIS _____

_____

_____

_____

WHAT DOES MY DOG NEED TO KNOW FOR THIS ADVENTURE? _____

_____

_____

_____

SUMMARY OF THE DAY _____

_____

_____

_____

_____

_____

_____

_____

_____

_____

FUN SCALE:

1 BISCUIT OF FUN   10 BISCUITS OF FUN

LEARN HOW TO PADDLEBOARD

2

Activities and skills we want to learn together

RUN A 5K

SWIM IN THE OCEAN

MASTER AN AGILITY COURSE

GO BIKING TOGETHER

1

_____

_____

_____

☐ COMPLETED

DATE

WHY WE WANT TO DO THIS _____

_____

_____

_____

WHAT DOES MY DOG NEED TO KNOW FOR THIS ADVENTURE? _____

_____

_____

_____

SUMMARY OF THE DAY _____

_____

_____

_____

_____

_____

_____

_____

_____

_____

FUN SCALE: 🦴 🦴 🦴 🦴 🦴 🦴 🦴 🦴 🦴 🦴

1 BISCUIT OF FUN   10 BISCUITS OF FUN

☐

COMPLETED

·········

DATE

2

WHY WE WANT TO DO THIS _____

_____

_____

_____

_____

WHAT DOES MY DOG NEED TO KNOW FOR THIS ADVENTURE? _____

_____

_____

_____

SUMMARY OF THE DAY _____

_____

_____

_____

_____

_____

_____

_____

_____

_____

FUN SCALE: 🦴 🦴 🦴 🦴 🦴 🦴 🦴 🦴 🦴 🦴

1 BISCUIT OF FUN   10 BISCUITS OF FUN

3 _____

☐
COMPLETED

DATE

WHY WE WANT TO DO THIS _____

_____

_____

_____

WHAT DOES MY DOG NEED TO KNOW FOR THIS ADVENTURE? _____

_____

_____

_____

SUMMARY OF THE DAY _____

_____

_____

_____

_____

_____

_____

_____

_____

FUN SCALE: 🦴 🦴 🦴 🦴 🦴 🦴 🦴 🦴 🦴 🦴

1 BISCUIT OF FUN   10 BISCUITS OF FUN

□

COMPLETED

_____

DATE

4

WHY WE WANT TO DO THIS

WHAT DOES MY DOG NEED TO KNOW FOR THIS ADVENTURE?

SUMMARY OF THE DAY

FUN SCALE:

1 BISCUIT OF FUN

10 BISCUITS OF FUN

5

_____

_____

☐

COMPLETED

DATE

WHY WE WANT TO DO THIS

_____

_____

_____

_____

WHAT DOES MY DOG NEED TO KNOW FOR THIS ADVENTURE?

_____

_____

_____

SUMMARY OF THE DAY

_____

_____

_____

_____

_____

_____

_____

_____

FUN SCALE:

1 BISCUIT OF FUN   10 BISCUITS OF FUN

☐

COMPLETED

_____

DATE

6

WHY WE WANT TO DO THIS _____

_____

_____

_____

WHAT DOES MY DOG NEED TO KNOW FOR THIS ADVENTURE? _____

_____

_____

_____

SUMMARY OF THE DAY _____

_____

_____

_____

_____

_____

_____

_____

_____

FUN SCALE: 🦴 🦴 🦴 🦴 🦴 🦴 🦴 🦴 🦴 🦴

1 BISCUIT OF FUN   10 BISCUITS OF FUN

7

_____

_____

_____

WHY WE WANT TO DO THIS

_____

_____

_____

WHAT DOES MY DOG NEED TO KNOW FOR THIS ADVENTURE?

_____

_____

_____

SUMMARY OF THE DAY

_____

_____

_____

_____

_____

_____

_____

_____

FUN SCALE:

1 BISCUIT OF FUN   10 BISCUITS OF FUN

COMPLETED

DATE

8

WHY WE WANT TO DO THIS

WHAT DOES MY DOG NEED TO KNOW FOR THIS ADVENTURE?

SUMMARY OF THE DAY

FUN SCALE:

1 BISCUIT OF FUN   10 BISCUITS OF FUN

9

☐
COMPLETED

DATE

WHY WE WANT TO DO THIS

WHAT DOES MY DOG NEED TO KNOW FOR THIS ADVENTURE?

SUMMARY OF THE DAY

FUN SCALE:

1 BISCUIT OF FUN
10 BISCUITS OF FUN

☐

COMPLETED

_____

DATE

10

_____

_____

_____

_____

WHY WE WANT TO DO THIS _____

_____

_____

_____

WHAT DOES MY DOG NEED TO KNOW FOR THIS ADVENTURE? _____

_____

_____

_____

SUMMARY OF THE DAY _____

_____

_____

_____

_____

_____

_____

_____

_____

FUN SCALE: 🦴 🦴 🦴 🦴 🦴 🦴 🦴 🦴 🦴 🦴

1 BISCUIT OF FUN   10 BISCUITS OF FUN

11

_____

_____

_____

WHY WE WANT TO DO THIS _____

_____

_____

_____

WHAT DOES MY DOG NEED TO KNOW FOR THIS ADVENTURE? _____

_____

_____

_____

SUMMARY OF THE DAY _____

_____

_____

_____

_____

_____

_____

_____

_____

_____

FUN SCALE:

1 BISCUIT OF FUN   10 BISCUITS OF FUN

RUN OFF LEASH IN THE MOUNTAINS

12

_____

_____

_____

WHY WE WANT TO DO THIS

_____

_____

_____

_____

WHAT DOES MY DOG NEED TO KNOW FOR THIS ADVENTURE?

_____

_____

_____

_____

SUMMARY OF THE DAY

_____

_____

_____

_____

_____

_____

_____

_____

_____

FUN SCALE:

1 BISCUIT OF FUN   10 BISCUITS OF FUN

☐ COMPLETED

_____

DATE

13

WHY WE WANT TO DO THIS _____

_____

_____

_____

WHAT DOES MY DOG NEED TO KNOW FOR THIS ADVENTURE? _____

_____

_____

_____

SUMMARY OF THE DAY _____

_____

_____

_____

_____

_____

_____

_____

_____

_____

FUN SCALE: 🦴 🦴 🦴 🦴 🦴 🦴 🦴 🦴 🦴 🦴

1 BISCUIT OF FUN   10 BISCUITS OF FUN

14 _____

WHY WE WANT TO DO THIS _____

_____

_____

_____

_____

WHAT DOES MY DOG NEED TO KNOW FOR THIS ADVENTURE? _____

_____

_____

_____

_____

SUMMARY OF THE DAY _____

_____

_____

_____

_____

_____

_____

_____

_____

_____

FUN SCALE:

1 BISCUIT OF FUN   10 BISCUITS OF FUN

☐

COMPLETED

_____

DATE

15

WHY WE WANT TO DO THIS _____

_____

_____

_____

_____

WHAT DOES MY DOG NEED TO KNOW FOR THIS ADVENTURE? _____

_____

_____

_____

SUMMARY OF THE DAY _____

_____

_____

_____

_____

_____

_____

_____

_____

_____

FUN SCALE: 🦴 🦴 🦴 🦴 🦴 🦴 🦴 🦴 🦴 🦴

1 BISCUIT OF FUN   10 BISCUITS OF FUN

16

_____

WHY WE WANT TO DO THIS

_____

WHAT DOES MY DOG NEED TO KNOW FOR THIS ADVENTURE?

_____

SUMMARY OF THE DAY

_____

FUN SCALE:

1 BISCUIT OF FUN   10 BISCUITS OF FUN

☐
COMPLETED

_____

DATE

17

WHY WE WANT TO DO THIS _____

_____

_____

_____

WHAT DOES MY DOG NEED TO KNOW FOR THIS ADVENTURE? _____

_____

_____

_____

SUMMARY OF THE DAY _____

_____

_____

_____

_____

_____

_____

_____

_____

_____

FUN SCALE:

1 BISCUIT OF FUN   10 BISCUITS OF FUN

18

_____
_____
_____

☐ COMPLETED

DATE

WHY WE WANT TO DO THIS
_____
_____
_____
_____

WHAT DOES MY DOG NEED TO KNOW FOR THIS ADVENTURE?
_____
_____
_____
_____

SUMMARY OF THE DAY
_____
_____
_____
_____
_____
_____
_____
_____
_____

FUN SCALE:

1 BISCUIT OF FUN   10 BISCUITS OF FUN

□
COMPLETED

_____

DATE

WHY WE WANT TO DO THIS _____

WHAT DOES MY DOG NEED TO KNOW FOR THIS ADVENTURE? _____

SUMMARY OF THE DAY _____

FUN SCALE:

1 BISCUIT OF FUN   10 BISCUITS OF FUN

20

_____

☐
COMPLETED

DATE

WHY WE WANT TO DO THIS

_____

WHAT DOES MY DOG NEED TO KNOW FOR THIS ADVENTURE?

_____

SUMMARY OF THE DAY

_____

FUN SCALE:

1 BISCUIT OF FUN   10 BISCUITS OF FUN

☐

COMPLETED

_____

DATE

_____
_____
_____

21

WHY WE WANT TO DO THIS _____

_____
_____
_____

WHAT DOES MY DOG NEED TO KNOW FOR THIS ADVENTURE? _____

_____
_____
_____

SUMMARY OF THE DAY _____

_____
_____
_____
_____
_____
_____
_____
_____
_____
_____

FUN SCALE:

1 BISCUIT OF FUN   10 BISCUITS OF FUN

22

☐

COMPLETED

DATE

WHY WE WANT TO DO THIS

WHAT DOES MY DOG NEED TO KNOW FOR THIS ADVENTURE?

SUMMARY OF THE DAY

FUN SCALE:

1 BISCUIT OF FUN   10 BISCUITS OF FUN

☐

COMPLETED

....

DATE

23

WHY WE WANT TO DO THIS

_____

_____

_____

_____

WHAT DOES MY DOG NEED TO KNOW FOR THIS ADVENTURE?

_____

_____

_____

SUMMARY OF THE DAY

_____

_____

_____

_____

_____

_____

_____

_____

FUN SCALE: 🦴 🦴 🦴 🦴 🦴 🦴 🦴 🦴 🦴 🦴

1 BISCUIT OF FUN   10 BISCUITS OF FUN

24

DATE

WHY WE WANT TO DO THIS

WHAT DOES MY DOG NEED TO KNOW FOR THIS ADVENTURE?

SUMMARY OF THE DAY

FUN SCALE:

1 BISCUIT OF FUN   10 BISCUITS OF FUN

☐

COMPLETED

....

DATE

25

_____
_____
_____
_____

WHY WE WANT TO DO THIS

_____
_____
_____
_____

WHAT DOES MY DOG NEED TO KNOW FOR THIS ADVENTURE?

_____
_____
_____
_____

SUMMARY OF THE DAY

_____
_____
_____
_____
_____
_____
_____
_____
_____

FUN SCALE: 🦴 🦴 🦴 🦴 🦴 🦴 🦴 🦴 🦴 🦴

1 BISCUIT OF FUN   10 BISCUITS OF FUN

TITLE IN SHEEP HERDING

3

Goals we want to achieve

STAR IN A PHOTO SHOOT

EARN AN AKC GOOD CITIZEN TITLE

BECOME A THERAPY DOG

ADOPT A SECOND DOG

1

_____

_____

_____

_____

☐

COMPLETED

DATE

WHY WE WANT TO DO THIS _____

_____

_____

_____

WHAT DOES MY DOG NEED TO KNOW FOR THIS ADVENTURE? _____

_____

_____

_____

SUMMARY OF THE DAY _____

_____

_____

_____

_____

_____

_____

_____

_____

FUN SCALE:

1 BISCUIT OF FUN   10 BISCUITS OF FUN

☐

COMPLETED

_____

DATE

2

WHY WE WANT TO DO THIS

_____

_____

_____

_____

WHAT DOES MY DOG NEED TO KNOW FOR THIS ADVENTURE?

_____

_____

_____

SUMMARY OF THE DAY

_____

_____

_____

_____

_____

_____

_____

_____

FUN SCALE: 🦴 🦴 🦴 🦴 🦴 🦴 🦴 🦴 🦴 🦴

1 BISCUIT OF FUN   10 BISCUITS OF FUN

3 _____

_____

_____

_____

WHY WE WANT TO DO THIS

_____

_____

_____

WHAT DOES MY DOG NEED TO KNOW FOR THIS ADVENTURE?

_____

_____

_____

SUMMARY OF THE DAY

_____

_____

_____

_____

_____

_____

_____

_____

FUN SCALE:

1 BISCUIT OF FUN   10 BISCUITS OF FUN

COMPLETED

_____

DATE

WHY WE WANT TO DO THIS _____

_____

_____

_____

WHAT DOES MY DOG NEED TO KNOW FOR THIS ADVENTURE? _____

_____

_____

_____

SUMMARY OF THE DAY _____

_____

_____

_____

_____

_____

_____

_____

_____

FUN SCALE:

1 BISCUIT OF FUN   10 BISCUITS OF FUN

5

_____

_____

_____

WHY WE WANT TO DO THIS

_____

_____

_____

_____

WHAT DOES MY DOG NEED TO KNOW FOR THIS ADVENTURE?

_____

_____

_____

_____

SUMMARY OF THE DAY

_____

_____

_____

_____

_____

_____

_____

_____

_____

FUN SCALE:

1 BISCUIT OF FUN   10 BISCUITS OF FUN

☐ COMPLETED

_____

DATE

6

WHY WE WANT TO DO THIS _____

_____

_____

_____

WHAT DOES MY DOG NEED TO KNOW FOR THIS ADVENTURE? _____

_____

_____

_____

SUMMARY OF THE DAY _____

_____

_____

_____

_____

_____

_____

_____

FUN SCALE: 🦴 🦴 🦴 🦴 🦴 🦴 🦴 🦴 🦴 🦴

1 BISCUIT OF FUN   10 BISCUITS OF FUN

7

_____

_____

_____

_____

☐

COMPLETED

_____

DATE

WHY WE WANT TO DO THIS _____

_____

_____

_____

_____

WHAT DOES MY DOG NEED TO KNOW FOR THIS ADVENTURE? _____

_____

_____

_____

_____

SUMMARY OF THE DAY _____

_____

_____

_____

_____

_____

_____

_____

_____

_____

FUN SCALE:

1 BISCUIT OF FUN

10 BISCUITS OF FUN

☐ COMPLETED

_____ DATE

8

WHY WE WANT TO DO THIS

WHAT DOES MY DOG NEED TO KNOW FOR THIS ADVENTURE?

SUMMARY OF THE DAY

FUN SCALE:

1 BISCUIT OF FUN   10 BISCUITS OF FUN

9. _____

_____

_____

DATE

WHY WE WANT TO DO THIS _____

_____

_____

_____

WHAT DOES MY DOG NEED TO KNOW FOR THIS ADVENTURE? _____

_____

_____

_____

SUMMARY OF THE DAY _____

_____

_____

_____

_____

_____

_____

_____

_____

FUN SCALE:

1 BISCUIT OF FUN   10 BISCUITS OF FUN

☐

COMPLETED

_____

DATE

10

WHY WE WANT TO DO THIS _____

_____

_____

_____

WHAT DOES MY DOG NEED TO KNOW FOR THIS ADVENTURE? _____

_____

_____

_____

SUMMARY OF THE DAY _____

_____

_____

_____

_____

_____

_____

_____

_____

FUN SCALE: 🦴 🦴 🦴 🦴 🦴 🦴 🦴 🦴 🦴 🦴

1 BISCUIT OF FUN   10 BISCUITS OF FUN

11

_____

_____

_____

WHY WE WANT TO DO THIS _____

_____

_____

_____

WHAT DOES MY DOG NEED TO KNOW FOR THIS ADVENTURE? _____

_____

_____

_____

SUMMARY OF THE DAY _____

_____

_____

_____

_____

_____

_____

_____

_____

_____

FUN SCALE:

1 BISCUIT OF FUN   10 BISCUITS OF FUN

BIKE 100 MILES IN A DAY

12

☐
COMPLETED

DATE

WHY WE WANT TO DO THIS

WHAT DOES MY DOG NEED TO KNOW FOR THIS ADVENTURE?

SUMMARY OF THE DAY

FUN SCALE:
1 BISCUIT OF FUN   10 BISCUITS OF FUN

□

COMPLETED

_____

DATE

13

WHY WE WANT TO DO THIS _____

_____

_____

_____

_____

WHAT DOES MY DOG NEED TO KNOW FOR THIS ADVENTURE? _____

_____

_____

_____

SUMMARY OF THE DAY _____

_____

_____

_____

_____

_____

_____

_____

_____

_____

FUN SCALE: 🦴 🦴 🦴 🦴 🦴 🦴 🦴 🦴 🦴 🦴

1 BISCUIT OF FUN   10 BISCUITS OF FUN

14

_____

_____

_____

☐

COMPLETED

DATE

WHY WE WANT TO DO THIS _____

_____

_____

_____

WHAT DOES MY DOG NEED TO KNOW FOR THIS ADVENTURE? _____

_____

_____

_____

SUMMARY OF THE DAY _____

_____

_____

_____

_____

_____

_____

_____

_____

_____

FUN SCALE:

1 BISCUIT OF FUN   10 BISCUITS OF FUN

☐

COMPLETED

_____

DATE

15

WHY WE WANT TO DO THIS _____

_____

_____

_____

WHAT DOES MY DOG NEED TO KNOW FOR THIS ADVENTURE? _____

_____

_____

_____

SUMMARY OF THE DAY _____

_____

_____

_____

_____

_____

_____

_____

FUN SCALE: 🦴 🦴 🦴 🦴 🦴 🦴 🦴 🦴 🦴 🦴

1 BISCUIT OF FUN   10 BISCUITS OF FUN

16

☐

COMPLETED

DATE

WHY WE WANT TO DO THIS

_____

WHAT DOES MY DOG NEED TO KNOW FOR THIS ADVENTURE?

_____

SUMMARY OF THE DAY

_____

FUN SCALE:

1 BISCUIT OF FUN   10 BISCUITS OF FUN

☐

COMPLETED

....

DATE

17

WHY WE WANT TO DO THIS

_____

_____

_____

_____

WHAT DOES MY DOG NEED TO KNOW FOR THIS ADVENTURE?

_____

_____

_____

SUMMARY OF THE DAY

_____

_____

_____

_____

_____

_____

_____

_____

FUN SCALE:

1 BISCUIT OF FUN   10 BISCUITS OF FUN

18

_____

_____

_____

☐

COMPLETED

DATE

WHY WE WANT TO DO THIS _____

_____

_____

_____

WHAT DOES MY DOG NEED TO KNOW FOR THIS ADVENTURE? _____

_____

_____

_____

SUMMARY OF THE DAY _____

_____

_____

_____

_____

_____

_____

_____

_____

FUN SCALE:

1 BISCUIT OF FUN   10 BISCUITS OF FUN

☐

COMPLETED

_____

DATE

19

WHY WE WANT TO DO THIS

_____

_____

_____

_____

WHAT DOES MY DOG NEED TO KNOW FOR THIS ADVENTURE?

_____

_____

_____

_____

SUMMARY OF THE DAY

_____

_____

_____

_____

_____

_____

_____

_____

_____

_____

FUN SCALE:

1 BISCUIT OF FUN   10 BISCUITS OF FUN

20

_____
_____
_____
_____

☐
COMPLETED

DATE

WHY WE WANT TO DO THIS _____
_____
_____
_____

WHAT DOES MY DOG NEED TO KNOW FOR THIS ADVENTURE? _____
_____
_____
_____

SUMMARY OF THE DAY _____
_____
_____
_____
_____
_____
_____
_____
_____

FUN SCALE: 🦴 🦴 🦴 🦴 🦴 🦴 🦴 🦴 🦴 🦴

1 BISCUIT OF FUN   10 BISCUITS OF FUN

☐

COMPLETED

DATE

WHY WE WANT TO DO THIS

WHAT DOES MY DOG NEED TO KNOW FOR THIS ADVENTURE?

SUMMARY OF THE DAY

FUN SCALE:

1 BISCUIT OF FUN

10 BISCUITS OF FUN

22

WHY WE WANT TO DO THIS

_____

_____

_____

_____

WHAT DOES MY DOG NEED TO KNOW FOR THIS ADVENTURE?

_____

_____

_____

_____

SUMMARY OF THE DAY

_____

_____

_____

_____

_____

_____

_____

_____

_____

FUN SCALE:

1 BISCUIT OF FUN   10 BISCUITS OF FUN

☐ COMPLETED

....

DATE

23

_____
_____
_____

WHY WE WANT TO DO THIS _____
_____
_____
_____
_____

WHAT DOES MY DOG NEED TO KNOW FOR THIS ADVENTURE? _____
_____
_____
_____

SUMMARY OF THE DAY _____
_____
_____
_____
_____
_____
_____
_____
_____
_____
_____

FUN SCALE: 🦴 🦴 🦴 🦴 🦴 🦴 🦴 🦴 🦴 🦴

1 BISCUIT OF FUN   10 BISCUITS OF FUN

24

☐
COMPLETED

DATE

WHY WE WANT TO DO THIS

WHAT DOES MY DOG NEED TO KNOW FOR THIS ADVENTURE?

SUMMARY OF THE DAY

FUN SCALE:

1 BISCUIT OF FUN   10 BISCUITS OF FUN

□

COMPLETED

....

DATE

25

WHY WE WANT TO DO THIS _____

_____

_____

_____

WHAT DOES MY DOG NEED TO KNOW FOR THIS ADVENTURE? _____

_____

_____

_____

SUMMARY OF THE DAY _____

_____

_____

_____

_____

_____

_____

_____

_____

FUN SCALE: 🦴 🦴 🦴 🦴 🦴 🦴 🦴 🦴 🦴 🦴

1 BISCUIT OF FUN   10 BISCUITS OF FUN

SPEND A WHOLE DAY SNUGGLING IN A HAMMOCK

4

Just because we can

ROLL IN THE BIGGEST MUD PUDDLE WE CAN FIND

EAT STEAK FOR BREAKFAST, LUNCH, AND DINNER

SWIM IN A POOL FILLED WITH TENNIS BALLS

DIG FOR BURIED TREASURE ON THE BEACH

1

_____

_____

_____

☐

COMPLETED

_____

DATE

WHY WE WANT TO DO THIS _____

_____

_____

_____

WHAT DOES MY DOG NEED TO KNOW FOR THIS ADVENTURE? _____

_____

_____

_____

SUMMARY OF THE DAY _____

_____

_____

_____

_____

_____

_____

_____

_____

FUN SCALE:

1 BISCUIT OF FUN   10 BISCUITS OF FUN

☐

COMPLETED

_____

DATE

2

WHY WE WANT TO DO THIS _____

_____

_____

_____

WHAT DOES MY DOG NEED TO KNOW FOR THIS ADVENTURE? _____

_____

_____

_____

SUMMARY OF THE DAY _____

_____

_____

_____

_____

_____

_____

_____

_____

FUN SCALE:

1 BISCUIT OF FUN   10 BISCUITS OF FUN

3

_____

☐

COMPLETED

_____

DATE

WHY WE WANT TO DO THIS _____

_____

_____

_____

WHAT DOES MY DOG NEED TO KNOW FOR THIS ADVENTURE? _____

_____

_____

_____

SUMMARY OF THE DAY _____

_____

_____

_____

_____

_____

_____

_____

_____

FUN SCALE:

🦴 🦴 🦴 🦴 🦴 🦴 🦴 🦴 🦴 🦴

1 BISCUIT OF FUN   10 BISCUITS OF FUN

☐

COMPLETED

....

DATE

4

WHY WE WANT TO DO THIS _____

_____

_____

_____

WHAT DOES MY DOG NEED TO KNOW FOR THIS ADVENTURE? _____

_____

_____

_____

SUMMARY OF THE DAY _____

_____

_____

_____

_____

_____

_____

_____

_____

FUN SCALE: 🦴 🦴 🦴 🦴 🦴 🦴 🦴 🦴 🦴 🦴

1 BISCUIT OF FUN   10 BISCUITS OF FUN

5 _____

_____

_____

☐
COMPLETED

....
DATE

WHY WE WANT TO DO THIS _____

_____

_____

_____

WHAT DOES MY DOG NEED TO KNOW FOR THIS ADVENTURE? _____

_____

_____

_____

SUMMARY OF THE DAY _____

_____

_____

_____

_____

_____

_____

_____

_____

_____

FUN SCALE:

1 BISCUIT OF FUN   10 BISCUITS OF FUN

☐

COMPLETED

....
DATE

_6_

WHY WE WANT TO DO THIS _____

_____

_____

_____

WHAT DOES MY DOG NEED TO KNOW FOR THIS ADVENTURE? _____

_____

_____

_____

SUMMARY OF THE DAY _____

_____

_____

_____

_____

_____

_____

_____

FUN SCALE: 🦴 🦴 🦴 🦴 🦴 🦴 🦴 🦴 🦴 🦴

1 BISCUIT OF FUN   10 BISCUITS OF FUN

7

☐
COMPLETED

DATE

WHY WE WANT TO DO THIS

WHAT DOES MY DOG NEED TO KNOW FOR THIS ADVENTURE?

SUMMARY OF THE DAY

FUN SCALE:

1 BISCUIT OF FUN

10 BISCUITS OF FUN

COMPLETED

DATE

WHY WE WANT TO DO THIS

WHAT DOES MY DOG NEED TO KNOW FOR THIS ADVENTURE?

SUMMARY OF THE DAY

FUN SCALE:

1 BISCUIT OF FUN

10 BISCUITS OF FUN

9

_____

_____

_____

☐

COMPLETED

_____

DATE

WHY WE WANT TO DO THIS _____

_____

_____

_____

WHAT DOES MY DOG NEED TO KNOW FOR THIS ADVENTURE? _____

_____

_____

_____

SUMMARY OF THE DAY _____

_____

_____

_____

_____

_____

_____

_____

_____

_____

FUN SCALE:

1 BISCUIT OF FUN

10 BISCUITS OF FUN

☐

COMPLETED

....

DATE

10

WHY WE WANT TO DO THIS

_____

_____

_____

_____

WHAT DOES MY DOG NEED TO KNOW FOR THIS ADVENTURE?

_____

_____

_____

SUMMARY OF THE DAY

_____

_____

_____

_____

_____

_____

_____

_____

FUN SCALE:

1 BISCUIT OF FUN   10 BISCUITS OF FUN

11

☐
COMPLETED

DATE

WHY WE WANT TO DO THIS

WHAT DOES MY DOG NEED TO KNOW FOR THIS ADVENTURE?

SUMMARY OF THE DAY

FUN SCALE:

1 BISCUIT OF FUN   10 BISCUITS OF FUN

BIRTHDAY STEAK

12

_____

_____

_____

_____

WHY WE WANT TO DO THIS _____

_____

_____

_____

WHAT DOES MY DOG NEED TO KNOW FOR THIS ADVENTURE? _____

_____

_____

_____

SUMMARY OF THE DAY _____

_____

_____

_____

_____

_____

_____

_____

_____

_____

FUN SCALE:

1 BISCUIT OF FUN   10 BISCUITS OF FUN

☐

COMPLETED

_____

DATE

13

WHY WE WANT TO DO THIS _____

_____

_____

_____

WHAT DOES MY DOG NEED TO KNOW FOR THIS ADVENTURE? _____

_____

_____

_____

SUMMARY OF THE DAY _____

_____

_____

_____

_____

_____

_____

_____

FUN SCALE:

1 BISCUIT OF FUN   10 BISCUITS OF FUN

14

_____

WHY WE WANT TO DO THIS _____

_____

_____

_____

WHAT DOES MY DOG NEED TO KNOW FOR THIS ADVENTURE? _____

_____

_____

_____

SUMMARY OF THE DAY _____

_____

_____

_____

_____

_____

_____

_____

_____

FUN SCALE:

1 BISCUIT OF FUN   10 BISCUITS OF FUN

COMPLETED

DATE

15

WHY WE WANT TO DO THIS

WHAT DOES MY DOG NEED TO KNOW FOR THIS ADVENTURE?

SUMMARY OF THE DAY

FUN SCALE:

1 BISCUIT OF FUN   10 BISCUITS OF FUN

16

_____

_____

_____

COMPLETED

_____
DATE

WHY WE WANT TO DO THIS _____

_____

_____

_____

WHAT DOES MY DOG NEED TO KNOW FOR THIS ADVENTURE? _____

_____

_____

_____

SUMMARY OF THE DAY _____

_____

_____

_____

_____

_____

_____

_____

_____

_____

FUN SCALE:

1 BISCUIT OF FUN   10 BISCUITS OF FUN

☐

COMPLETED

DATE

17

WHY WE WANT TO DO THIS

_____

WHAT DOES MY DOG NEED TO KNOW FOR THIS ADVENTURE?

_____

SUMMARY OF THE DAY

_____

FUN SCALE:

1 BISCUIT OF FUN   10 BISCUITS OF FUN

18

☐

COMPLETED

....

DATE

WHY WE WANT TO DO THIS

_____

_____

_____

_____

WHAT DOES MY DOG NEED TO KNOW FOR THIS ADVENTURE?

_____

_____

_____

_____

SUMMARY OF THE DAY

_____

_____

_____

_____

_____

_____

_____

_____

_____

_____

FUN SCALE:

1 BISCUIT OF FUN   10 BISCUITS OF FUN

☐

COMPLETED

_____
_____
_____
_____

19

DATE

WHY WE WANT TO DO THIS _____

_____
_____
_____
_____

WHAT DOES MY DOG NEED TO KNOW FOR THIS ADVENTURE? _____

_____
_____
_____

SUMMARY OF THE DAY _____

_____
_____
_____
_____
_____
_____
_____
_____
_____

FUN SCALE: 🦴 🦴 🦴 🦴 🦴 🦴 🦴 🦴 🦴 🦴

1 BISCUIT OF FUN   10 BISCUITS OF FUN

20

☐ COMPLETED

DATE

WHY WE WANT TO DO THIS

WHAT DOES MY DOG NEED TO KNOW FOR THIS ADVENTURE?

SUMMARY OF THE DAY

FUN SCALE:

1 BISCUIT OF FUN

10 BISCUITS OF FUN

☐

COMPLETED

....
DATE

21

WHY WE WANT TO DO THIS

WHAT DOES MY DOG NEED TO KNOW FOR THIS ADVENTURE?

SUMMARY OF THE DAY

FUN SCALE:

22

COMPLETED

DATE

WHY WE WANT TO DO THIS

WHAT DOES MY DOG NEED TO KNOW FOR THIS ADVENTURE?

SUMMARY OF THE DAY

FUN SCALE:

1 BISCUIT OF FUN

10 BISCUITS OF FUN

☐

COMPLETED

....

DATE

23

WHY WE WANT TO DO THIS _____

_____

_____

_____

WHAT DOES MY DOG NEED TO KNOW FOR THIS ADVENTURE? _____

_____

_____

_____

SUMMARY OF THE DAY _____

_____

_____

_____

_____

_____

_____

_____

_____

FUN SCALE:

1 BISCUIT OF FUN   10 BISCUITS OF FUN

24

WHY WE WANT TO DO THIS

WHAT DOES MY DOG NEED TO KNOW FOR THIS ADVENTURE?

SUMMARY OF THE DAY

FUN SCALE:

1 BISCUIT OF FUN   10 BISCUITS OF FUN

□ COMPLETED

DATE

25

WHY WE WANT TO DO THIS _____

_____

_____

_____

WHAT DOES MY DOG NEED TO KNOW FOR THIS ADVENTURE? _____

_____

_____

_____

SUMMARY OF THE DAY _____

_____

_____

_____

_____

_____

_____

_____

_____

FUN SCALE: 🦴 🦴 🦴 🦴 🦴 🦴 🦴 🦴 🦴 🦴

1 BISCUIT OF FUN   10 BISCUITS OF FUN

SHARE YOUR LIST
#NoDogLeftAtHome

FOLLOW OUR ADVENTURES
@SUP_WITH_PUP

Made in the USA
Columbia, SC
02 February 2019